Comprehension Teachers' Book 2

Contents

Part one

INTRODUCTION	2
STRUCTURE AND COMPONENTS	3
HOW TO USE KEY COMPREHENSION	3
READING COMPREHENSION TERMINOLOGY	5
Reading strategies	5
Comprehension skills: literal, deductive, inferential and evaluative understanding	5
RANGE OF QUESTION FORMS	7
TEACHING COMPREHENSION SKILLS	8
KEY COMPREHENSION AND THE NATIONAL CURRICULA	10
Key Comprehension and National Curricula tests	10
National Curriculum for England	11
English Language 5-14 Curriculum (Scotland)	12
Northern Ireland Curriculum for English	13
English in the National Curriculum in Wales	13
BIBLIOGRAPHY	14
RECORD KEEPING	15
Class record sheet	16
Pupil record sheet	17

Part two

INTRODUCTION	18
ANSWERS, MARK SCHEME AND EXTENSION ACTIVITIES	begin on 19

PART ONE

Introduction

> To read with fluency, accuracy, understanding and enjoyment, pupils should be taught to use a range of strategies to make sense of what they read.
> *(Revised National Curriculum for English in England 1999)*

> All teachers know that pupils become successful readers by learning to use a range of strategies to get at the meaning of a text.
> *(The National Literacy Strategy Framework for Teaching, 2001)*

> Learning to read accurately and with discrimination becomes increasingly important as pupils move through their education … [Pupils] should be helped to develop their own tastes in imaginative literature and non-fiction and at the same time to gain confidence in writing and speaking about them … The importance of meaning should be stressed at all stages …
> *(Scottish 5–14 Guidelines for English Language, 1991)*

> Pupils should be given opportunities to develop as enthusiastic, independent and reflective readers.
> *(English in the National Curriculum in Wales, 2000)*

> Pupils should develop the ability to read, understand and engage with various types of text for enjoyment and learning.
> *(Revised Northern Ireland Curriculum, 1996)*

The reading skills described above are those that every primary teacher aims to foster, and it is these skills that the Key Comprehension series targets.

Key Comprehension comprises five Pupils' Books and five accompanying Teachers' Handbooks, covering Years 2–6/Primary 2–7. The series helps to prepare pupils for the reading comprehension components of national Standard Assessment Tasks/National Tests (Scotland), and may also be used to prepare pupils for the comprehension components of 11+ entry tests in English to grammar and independent schools.

The Key Comprehension Starter Book is aimed at pupils in Year 2 (with substantial Year 1 revision)/Primary 2–3. It is targeted at England and Wales National Curriculum Levels 2–3, Scottish 5–14 Curriculum Level A and Northern Ireland Curriculum Levels 1–2.

Book 1 is aimed at pupils in Year 3/Primary 4. It is targeted at England and Wales National Curriculum Levels 2–4, Scottish 5–14 Curriculum Levels A–B and Northern Ireland Curriculum Levels 1–3.

Book 2 is aimed at pupils in Year 4/Primary 5. It is targeted at England and Wales National Curriculum Levels 3–5, Scottish 5–14 Curriculum Levels B–C and Northern Ireland Curriculum Levels 2–4.

Book 3 is aimed at pupils in Year 5/Primary 6. It is targeted at England and Wales National Curriculum Levels 3–6, Scottish 5–14 Curriculum Levels C–D and Northern Ireland Curriculum Levels 3–5.

Book 4 is aimed at pupils in Year 6/Primary 7. It is targeted at England and Wales National Curriculum Levels 4–7, Scottish 5–14 Curriculum Levels D–E and Northern Ireland Curriculum Levels 4–6.

Structure and components

Key Comprehension Book 2 contains thirty-seven self-contained Units of work. Each Unit consists of a short passage of text followed by a series of questions which test the children's understanding of the text.

The texts are taken from a wide range of sources and are lively and stimulating. Care has been taken to reflect the pupils' own experience and to engage their interest. In accordance with Curriculum guidelines, the genres represented include modern and well-established children's fiction, fables, myths, information texts and transactional material.

The questions are designed to encourage close and accurate reading of the texts and to foster an understanding of implicit as well as explicit meaning. The activities gradually become more demanding as the book progresses. The pupils' ability to skim and to scan, to order and to summarise, to pinpoint and to synthesise information is thus developed throughout the book.

For each Unit, the Teachers' Handbook provides answers to the questions, a breakdown of the comprehension skills tested in the activity, suggested cross-curricular links, a suggested mark scheme and ideas for extension work. These extension activities are often open-ended and offer a range of written assignments in a variety of genres, as well as comprehension questions of greater complexity, and related language work.

The Teachers' Handbook also contains a commentary on the range of reading and teaching strategies that are needed to develop comprehension skills, national curricula correlation information, pupil and class record sheets and a Bibliography containing details of the sources of texts for further reading.

How to use Key Comprehension

Units are arranged in order of gradually increasing difficulty and, generally speaking, are intended to be tackled in the order arranged. However, each Unit is self-contained to allow flexibility so teachers may choose to take some Units out of order if a particular topic, genre or question form is relevant to current class work.

Teachers will find that some children who are confident, independent readers are happy to tackle the Units with the minimum of teacher intervention. Others, however, will need considerable support and guidance before this stage is reached. Most children will benefit if the teacher talks through the activity first and explains exactly what they are being asked to do. If the children's own reading is hesitant, they will be helped by the teacher reading the passage to them and thereby arousing their attention and interest.

Although a prolonged discussion at the end of the reading would be inappropriate, it is a good opportunity to deal with the children's questions, pose a few tactical ones in anticipation of the printed ones that follow and perhaps discuss relevant aspects of the illustrations. When the children are comfortable with the passage, it can be helpful if the text is "put back together again" by being read aloud a second time.

The teacher may then wish to read through the questions with the children and discuss answers. In this informal atmosphere, the teacher is able to encourage and to prompt, and to praise warmly when thoughtful answers (firmly based on the text) are given. Children must be encouraged to pay close attention to the exact wording of the question, and to consider it in its entirety before attempting an answer. Teachers can also help children search the text for the answer, and gently dismiss hopefully inventive responses.

As their confidence grows, children will be happy working together in pairs and in groups, reading the passage and questions themselves. Teachers will need to be on hand to support, guide and focus attention when appropriate. Collaborative activities can be very supportive when the members are well matched and each contributes thoughtfully, but teachers need to be vigilant to spot those who are taking without giving, and simply copying the answers down.

Sequencing, cloze and multiple-choice activities lend themselves easily to consensus decisions, and can be self-marked by the group from answers given in the Teachers' Handbook. This self-marking can be a learning activity too if the group returns to the text to establish the validity of the given answer where the group had made a wrong decision. Units where answers have to be given in the pupils' own words are sometimes less satisfactory as collaborative activities unless the children are sophisticated enough to benefit from the discussion and are happy to express themselves on paper independently. Pupils will find it more difficult to assess their own answer here by comparison with the suggested answers because wording may vary considerably.

The Teachers' Handbook allocates a full page to each Unit and provides suggested answers and extension activities. Teachers may wish to give children a photocopy of the relevant page and allow children to check their own work alongside the suggested answers before going on to work on the extension activities provided on the same sheet.

Key Comprehension can be used to give children an opportunity to work in controlled conditions from time to time in preparation for the National Curriculum Reading Comprehension tests (England, Wales and Northern Ireland) and 5–14 National Tests (Scotland). Children unused to working on their own and in silence can be disadvantaged and unnecessarily stressed during such unfamiliar formal tests. Units from Key Comprehension can be used for individual silent practice, and pupils can become accustomed to the rules of "no conferring" and "no asking questions". They can also become familiar with working against the clock if the practice is timed.

Lastly, the Units form a useful basis for homework assignments where parental involvement can be guided and encouraged.

Reading comprehension terminology

Reading strategies

Skimming, scanning and detailed reading are essential strategies for effective information retrieval and for full understanding and exploration of texts. All three strategies are developed during the course of Key Comprehension Book 2.

Skimming and scanning are terms much in use since the advent of the national curricula. They are often used rather vaguely but are, in fact, two distinct reading strategies.

Skimming

Skimming involves reading swiftly through text in order to register the general outline (the gist) and omitting the detail. This gives the reader an overview of the material and an idea of where in the text, roughly, to find passages for closer reading later.

Scanning

Scanning involves rapid but focused reading of text, in order to locate specific information, e.g. looking for particular details such as dates, names, certain types of words, and so on.

Detailed reading

Detailed reading involves reading text slowly and accurately in order to reflect upon the structure, purpose, content and tone of the text. The reader reads attentively, "listening" carefully to what the writer is saying.

When tackling the thirty-seven Units in Book 2, pupils will have to employ skimming, scanning and detailed reading techniques on a regular basis. The questions direct pupils back to the text in order to find the answers. Pupils need to be told that referring back to the text is expected *(and is not cheating!)*. Reading comprehension is not a memory test but an exercise in information retrieval and understanding.

Comprehension skills: literal, deductive, inferential and evaluative understanding

Key Comprehension Book 2 develops pupils' understanding of what they have read at several levels. The questions in the Units require deductive, inferential and evaluative understanding as well as literal understanding. These questions are designed to encourage pupils to read between the lines and interpret what they have read.

A wide variety of question forms is used to elicit a full range of responses requiring all these types of understanding.

Literal

Literal responses demonstrate the ability to understand the surface meaning of a text and to select information accurately from the text in answer to a question.
For example:

Question:	In which country would you see bee humming birds flying around? (Unit 7)
Answer:	*You would see bee humming birds in Cuba.*

Deductive

Deductive responses demonstrate the ability to reach a logical conclusion by drawing on personal experience from beyond the immediate context of the passage.
For example:

Question:	How do we know that the boys weren't at all sorry for what they had done? (Unit 19)
Answer:	*We know they weren't sorry because they just laughed.*

Inferential

Inferential responses demonstrate the ability to reach a logical conclusion on the basis of information given.
For example:

Question:	How did the Hungry Wolf try to trick them into opening the door the first time he knocked? (Unit 11)
Answer:	*He pretended he was their mother and said he wanted to give them pocket money.*

Evaluative

Evaluative responses demonstrate the ability to appraise, to form judgements and to weigh the evidence and its implications.
For example:

Question:	If you were Vera, what would you say to cheer Snap up? (Unit 10)
Answer:	*Open. Reward any sensible answers. Vera is sensible, practical and motherly. She is likely to tell him that she likes him just as he is; that breathing fire will come in good time; that if he cries he will never be able to breathe fire, etc.*

Range of question forms

The following chart summarises the range of question forms used in each Unit of work in Key Comprehension Book 2.

	cloze	sentence completion	sequencing	true or false	multiple choice	answering in sentences
UNIT 1	•					
UNIT 2			•			
UNIT 3				•		
UNIT 4	•	•				
UNIT 5					•	
UNIT 6				•	•	•
UNIT 7						•
UNIT 8				•		
UNIT 9			•			
UNIT 10						•
UNIT 11						•
UNIT 12						•
UNIT 13						•
UNIT 14					•	
UNIT 15						•
UNIT 16						•
UNIT 17						•
UNIT 18						•
UNIT 19						•
UNIT 20					•	
UNIT 21	•					
UNIT 22						•
UNIT 23					•	
UNIT 24				•		
UNIT 25						•
UNIT 26						•
UNIT 27						•
UNIT 28					•	•
UNIT 29					•	
UNIT 30						•
UNIT 31		•				
UNIT 32						•
UNIT 33				•		
UNIT 34		•				•
UNIT 35				•		
UNIT 36						•
UNIT 37						•

Teaching comprehension skills

The national curricula, the *National Literacy Strategy Framework for Teaching* and good teaching practice, enshrine the belief that comprehension skills can be taught.

> To read with fluency, accuracy, understanding and enjoyment, pupils should be taught to use a range of strategies to make sense of what they read.
> *(Revised National Curriculum for English in England 1999)*

> The importance of meaning should be stressed at all stages. The activity of reading should take place, wherever possible, in an appropriate context, and it should be concerned with the gaining of meaning from a suitable text.
> *(Scottish 5–14 Guidelines for English Language, 1991)*

> All teachers know that pupils become successful readers by learning to use a range of strategies to get at the meaning of a text.
> *(The National Literacy Strategy Framework for Teaching, 2001)*

> Pupils should be given opportunities to read extensively for their own interest and pleasure, and for information, using progressively more challenging and demanding texts.
> *(English in the National Curriculum in Wales, 2000)*

> Pupils should develop the ability to read, understand and engage with various types of text for enjoyment and learning.
> *(Revised Northern Ireland Curriculum, 1996)*

So how can such relatively sophisticated skills be taught and developed?
What exactly can the teacher in the classroom do?

It is helpful to realise that understanding a text and answering accurately questions based on it involve a cluster of acquired skills:
1 detailed reading
2 search reading (skimming and scanning)
3 retrieval (identification and selection)
4 communication (speaking/writing)

Let us look more closely at each of these.

1 Development of detailed reading skills

Detailed reading (without skipping) gives the reader a clear grasp of the narrative. It enables the reader to know what the text is about, although more than one reading may be necessary to unlock the meaning fully.

Children can be helped to develop their detailed reading skills by answering questions, both orally and on paper, as teachers have long known. In the early stages a great deal of reading through the passages in the Units with the pupils may well be necessary. Dialogue and discussion, reading and talking about what is being read, help to focus a child's attention on the meaning of the words he or she may well have been reading fluently but without engagement. Children can be prompted by a supportive teacher to return to the text just read to find the right answer to a question. Such questioning and this textual referral help to encourage focused, attentive and reflective reading.

It will also be useful to return to the text after the written answers have been completed to establish why some answers were incorrect or incomplete.

Detailed reading of the text is the key to understanding it. Needless to say, detailed reading of the questions is also very important.

2 Development of search reading skills (skimming and scanning)

When a child has an overview of a text, search reading skills are needed to locate quickly information required to answer a question. The child will know that the information is there somewhere but will need to be able to read through quickly to find it (skimming) and scrutinise when found (scanning).

The ability to skim over the surface of a text in search of information is a skill that children will probably not develop for themselves without encouragement. Many children, even at secondary level, have only one reading speed when tackling printed text.

Children can be encouraged to skim familiar texts by having small-group or whole-class skimming races. The teacher poses challenges such as "Find the place where it says in the passage that David has blue eyes". Winners have to put a finger on the right place in the text. It is wise to allow several children to raise their other hand triumphantly but then to intervene and show the rest before embarking on another search.

Scanning races yield information as well as location. The challenge above would be re-phrased as "Find the place in the passage where it tells us what colour David's eyes are". Winners would have to be able to locate the place in the text and retrieve the information. Children who simply remember the information get no credit here! The exercise is to *locate* the information with maximum speed.

3 Development of retrieval skills

The questions in the Key Comprehension series have been carefully devised to test (in a variety of forms) literal, deductive, inferential and evaluative understanding.

Questions testing *literal* understanding will simply require children to retrieve the relevant information from the text. The clues will be lying on the surface of the text. Once children have become used to referring back to the text for the information they need (and not relying on memory alone and not making up fanciful answers), this type of question should present no great difficulties. Children should enjoy locating and retrieving the answer.

Retrieving implicit meaning by *deduction* or *inference* is much more difficult, and children need to be helped to read between the lines. Questions targeting implicit meaning will be phrased along these lines: "How do you know that Sarah is the eldest child in the family?"; "Why do you think Tom feels so sad?" Children will be helped by gentle support here as they look for hidden clues. It does help to think of deductive and inferential retrieval skills as detective work! Plenty of practice is offered in Key Comprehension and children will gain much by working in pairs and small groups and exchanging their ideas as they discuss the text. Such discussions can be monitored by the teacher who can steer them away from unprofitable avenues and aim them in the right direction with some judicious questions. If children later have access to the answers in the Teachers' Handbook, they can see for themselves points in the given answers that they may have overlooked.

Occasionally *evaluative* answers are invited, requiring children to express an opinion which must be supported by close reference to the textual evidence. Such questions are open-ended and all pupils will have something valid to say. More able pupils will have the opportunity to marshal a cogent argument and to develop a view.

Children will meet a wide variety of question forms in the Units and it can be helpful to alert them to the demands each form presents. In *cloze* activities, children should be reminded that they need to read right to the end of the sentence before supplying the missing word. Some children attempt to fill the gap as soon as they reach it, not realising that the sentence as a whole provides the necessary contextual clues.

In *sequencing* activities, children need to be assured that there is one best ordering of the parts within the completed whole. They can be guided to spot sequential clues such as "Begin by ...", "next" and "finally", for example. They must make a logical and not a random choice in sequencing.

In *sentence completion*, what is added must fit syntactically and must complete the sense of the sentence satisfactorily. The completed sentence must be accurate when cross-referenced with the text. The temptation must be resisted to add any random ending that happens to occur to the child.

Children should be warned that *true/false* activities may well lay traps for the unwary reader. Slight but significant variations of wording may render one choice unacceptable although very close to the truth. Children can be warned not to fall into the trap.

With *multiple-choice* activities distracters may well be included that are very nearly the answer required. Great vigilance is necessary and all the possible choices should be considered carefully before a decision is made. It can be helpful to eliminate any obviously incorrect statements and then to concentrate on choosing the right answer from the statements that remain.

When children are *answering in their own words*, they should be reminded not to lift material straight from the passage but to answer the question clearly in their own way. Sometimes there is more than one point to be made. Children should make sure they have included all that is relevant in their answer.

4 Developing communication skills

Whether children discuss a reading comprehension or write their answers in carefully controlled conditions, they are developing communication skills. In pair work and in small group discussions, ideas should be shared courteously and productively, and the quality of the reading comprehension shown can be assessed by the monitoring teacher.

Answering reading comprehension questions by writing the answers can be a very challenging exercise for children with limited writing skills. It is for this reason that a variety of approaches is used to familiarise them with the kinds of structures useful when they come to answer questions in their own words.

Sometimes they are asked to copy out and complete a sentence (cloze and sentence completion); sometimes they have to select and write out a sentence from a pair or group in answer to a question (true/false, multiple choice); sometimes they have to write out sentences and captions in a logical order (sequencing). As the series progresses, they are expected to answer more questions in their own words, although more supportive exercises (from the writing point of view) are interspersed with these throughout the series.

Reading comprehension is traditionally tested by the writing of answers to questions. The development of writing skills will be encouraged not only by answering the questions in each of the Units but also by attempting the many varied extension activities in the Teachers' Handbook.

Teaching reading comprehension skills is an on-going classroom activity not, of course, confined to the English lesson. Such skills are vital if our children are to be enabled as enthusiastic, independent and reflective readers, as we would wish each one of them to be.

Key Comprehension and the national curricula

Key Comprehension and national curricula tests

Teachers may wish to use Key Comprehension Units formally in the classroom as preparation for National Curriculum Reading Comprehension tests (England, Wales and Northern Ireland) and 5–14 National Tests (Scotland).

Key Comprehension is a flexible resource and the Units may usefully be worked in controlled conditions as children become more confident about working individually and independently of teacher intervention. For some children, who are used only to working in pairs or groups, the experience of formally conducted tests can be a frightening one. Timed activities or conventions forbidding them to ask for help can be unfamiliar and bewildering.

Key Comprehension offers the opportunity of controlled practice in a supportive environment where the experience can be talked through beforehand and discussed afterwards. The overall task will gradually become familiar and the conventions understood. Children will be better prepared for formal tests if they have been given the opportunity from time to time of writing and working independently and quietly.

National Curriculum for England

The Key Stage 2 Programme of Study for Reading sets out the knowledge, skills and understanding that should be taught through a range of literature and non-fiction and non-literary texts. Key Comprehension is directed at nurturing the skills of reading a range of texts with fluency, accuracy and understanding, and thus the activities provide ideal support for the Curriculum.

The following chart draws on key phrases and concepts from the Reading Programme of Study for Key Stage 2, as set out in *English in the National Curriculum* (HMSO 1999).

PROGRAMME OF STUDY REFERENCE

Range of reading
To read with fluency, accuracy, understanding and enjoyment, pupils should be taught to:
2a use inference and deduction
2b look for meaning beyond the literal
3a scan texts to find information
3b skim for gist and overall impression
3c obtain specific information through detailed reading
To develop understanding and appreciation of literary texts, pupils should be taught to:
4a recognise the choice, use and effect of figurative language, vocabulary and patterns of language

Literature
The range should include:
a a range of modern fiction by significant children's authors
b long-established children's fiction
c a range of good-quality modern poetry
d classic poetry
e texts drawn from a variety of cultures and traditions
f myths, legends and traditional stories
g playscripts.

Non-fiction and non-literary texts
The range should include
a diaries, autobiographies, biographies, letters
b print and ICT-based reference and information materials
c newspapers, magazines, articles, leaflets, brochures, advertisements.

KEY COMPREHENSION BOOK 2

Reading strategies and understanding tested
Activities target reading texts for understanding: comprehension questions require literal, deductive, inferential and evaluative responses, requiring pupils to refer back to the text, skimming and scanning to identify and retrieve information. Activities include questions which focus specifically on figurative language and vocabulary. Notes in the Teachers' Handbook identify the types of understanding tested by each question. Questions ask for answers written in complete sentences to encourage development of appropriate Standard English writing in a formal context.

Extension activities in the Teachers' Handbook offer suggestions for follow-up work including discussion ideas and open-ended activities.

Literature
Texts include recent, established and traditional fiction, poetry and plays. There are texts from other cultures as well as those with familiar, fantasy and historical settings There is also a range of poetry forms including shape, haiku and limerick. Texts of increasing difficulty, both in length and vocabulary, enable children to be challenged in their developing ability to comprehend a range of literature.

Non-fiction and non-literary texts
Texts include a variety of non-fiction genres – e.g. instructions, explanation, alphabetical text, report, persuasive text, recount – and styles – e.g. dictionary, letter, leaflet, newspaper article, graph, biography. Illustrations, photographs and other visual information are included and are integral to the development of comprehension skills.

Scottish 5–14 Guidelines for English Language

Key Comprehension encourages children to read for meaning and with understanding and thus supports the Scottish 5–14 Guidelines for English Language (1991). The following chart draws on key phrases and concepts from the Reading Programmes of Study Introduction and the Reading Attainment Targets for Levels B and C.

PROGRAMME OF STUDY REFERENCE	KEY COMPREHENSION BOOK 2
AT Strand **Reading to reflect on the writer's ideas and craft** **Level B** Read straightforward texts and in discussion and writing show that they understand the main ideas. **Level C** Read a variety of straightforward texts, and in discussion and writing show that they understand the main and supporting ideas and can draw conclusions from the text where appropriate.	Key Comprehension provides a structured framework for written comprehension tasks. Extension activities in the Teachers' Handbook offer suggestions for follow-up work including discussion ideas and open-ended activities. Notes in the Teachers' Handbook identify the types of understanding tested by each question.
(**Introduction to PoS**) Learning to read accurately and with discrimination becomes increasingly important as pupils move through their education. The importance of meaning should be stressed at all stages.	Key Comprehension activities focus on developing reading with understanding.
As texts become more complex and various in form, the teacher needs to deploy a widening range of techniques such as sequencing, prediction, cloze procedure, evaluating the text, making deductions, marking text, comparing and contrasting different texts.	A variety of comprehension question forms and techniques is used including sequencing, cloze procedure, literal, inferential, deductive and evaluative question forms.
Reading activities should demand that pupils show an overall grasp of a text, an understanding of specific details and how they contribute to the whole, make inferences, supply supporting evidence.	Questions require pupils to read closely and use skimming and scanning techniques to retrieve specific information.
In teaching reading through all stages, in ways appropriate to pupils' ages and attainment, the teacher can focus on texts: *before reading,* by priming pupils for the task, for example by alerting them to unfamiliar content or ideas; by directing them into the task; *during and after reading,*	Texts increase in difficulty gradually. The Teachers' Handbook suggests ways of introducing the formal comprehension activities, how to encourage the children to tackle the tasks and how to follow up the work.
by providing questions which ask for literal, inferential and evaluative responses; by asking them to demonstrate understanding by doing or speaking; by asking readers to use the text as a model for their own writing.	Activities include literal, inferential and evaluative questions designed to develop comprehension skills.

12

Northern Ireland Curriculum for English

The curriculum states that: "Pupils should develop the ability to read, understand and engage with various types of text for enjoyment and learning." *(Programme of Study: Reading)*

Key Comprehension supports this aim by targeting reading for understanding using a wide range of texts and question types.

The following chart draws on key phrases and concepts from the Reading Programme of Study for lower Key Stage 2 as set out in the *Northern Ireland Curriculum for English (1996)*.

NI CURRICULUM REFERENCE	KEY COMPREHENSION BOOK 2
a listening to and understanding a range of texts	Understanding of a range of interesting and enjoyable texts is tested through a structured comprehension programme.
b/c participating in shared reading experiences; exploring stories and other texts with the teacher **f** discussing and interpreting texts they have read	The Pupils' Book lends itself to a range of classroom applications, from formal comprehension through to varied extension ideas in the Teachers' Handbook including discussion points and open-ended activities.
i justifying their responses logically by inference, deduction and reference to evidence within the text	Questions requiring literal, deductive, inferential and evaluative responses are included. Question types are fully referenced in the Teachers' Handbook. Questions require pupils to locate specific details in texts, to interpret what they have read and to demonstrate their understanding.

English in the National Curriculum in Wales

The curriculum requires children to read a wide range of information texts, fiction, poetry and playscripts, of increasing complexity. Key Comprehension supports these requirements by providing a wide range of graded texts, representing different genres and becoming progressively more challenging throughout the book.

WELSH CURRICULUM REFERENCE	KEY COMPREHENSION BOOK 2
2 read extensively for their own interest and pleasure using progressively more challenging and demanding texts. 4 read and use a wide range of sources of information 6 read a wide range of literature	Key Comprehension includes texts representing many of the required genres and text types including a range of information texts, traditional and modern fiction and poetry, and playscripts, of increasing complexity.

Bibliography

The texts used in Key Comprehension Book 2 are taken from the following sources:

Fiction

Walpole, Syd Holt, A World's Work Children's Book (Unit 1)

Jellybaby and Other Problem Pets, Linda Jennings, Puffin Books (Unit 5)

I Am Better Than You, Robert Lopshire, World's Work Ltd, The Windmill Press (Unit 6)

Sally, Dick King-Smith, Ginn & Company (Unit 8)

Snap, the Superhero, Stan Cullimore, Piccadilly Press (Unit 10)

Mrs Goat and Her Seven Little Kids, Tony Ross, Andersen Press (Unit 11)

Mrs Cockle's Cat, Philippa Pearce, Viking Kestrel (Unit 13)

Beware, Princess!, Mary Hoffman, William Heinemann (Unit 16)

Aesop's Fables, Dyma-Gymru Publications Ltd (Unit 17)

"Uninvited ghosts", Penelope Lively, from *A Treasury of Stories for Eight-year-olds*,
    ed. Edward and Nancy Blishen, Kingfisher Books (Unit 18)

The Magic Finger, Roald Dahl, Puffin Books (Unit 19)

The Marble Crusher, Michael Morpurgo, William Heinemann (Unit 25)

Dilly Dinosaur, Detective, Tony Bradman, William Heinemann (Unit 26)

"The flood" by Ruth Ainsworth, from *A Sackful of Stories for Eight-year-olds*, ed. Pat Thomson,
Corgi (Unit 30)

The Angel of Nitshill Road (play), Anne Fine, Ginn & Company (Unit 32)

Friend or Foe, Michael Morpurgo, Mammoth (Unit 37)

Poems

"Life's not been the same in my family" by Jack Pretlusky from *Something Big Has Been Here*,
    Heinemann (Unit 20)

"Our playground" by Colin West, from *Tough Toffee*, ed. David Orme, Lions (Unit 23)

"Cello" by Richard Lester, from *O Frabjous Day*! ed. Sandy Brownjohn, Ginn & Company (Unit 34)

"Drought" by Accabre Huntley, from *Chasing the Sun*, ed. Sally Bacon, Simon & Schuster Young
Books (Unit 36)

Non-fiction

Starting Technology: Machines, John Williams, Wayland Publishers Ltd (Unit 2)

How to Look After Your Rabbit, Colin and Jacqui Hawkins, Walker Books Ltd (Unit 3)

Science in the Kitchen, Rebecca Heddle, Usborne Publishing Ltd (Unit 4)

New Caribbean Junior Reader 2, Ginn & Company (Unit 7)

"Making nettle paper" based on *Simple Chemistry*, John and Dorothy Paull, Ladybird Junior
    Science (Unit 9)

The Spotter's Guide to Animals, Tracks and Signs, Alfred Leutscher, Puffin Books (Unit 12)

Devon County Libraries children's guide, Devon County Council (Unit 14)

"Your bike", based on *Bicycle Encyclopedia*, Ginn & Company (Unit 15)

"Years of compulsory education" from The Guinness European Data Book, Guinness
    Publishing (Unit 21)

Glass, Hazel Songhurst, Wayland Publishers Ltd (Unit 22)

"Boy attacked by mastiff" article from *Early Times Newspapers*, 23 December 1993 –
    5 January 1994 (Unit 24)

Castles: A Guide for Young People, Hugh Gregor, Macmillan for the Department of the
    Environment, HMSO (Unit 27)

Hedgehogs, Joanna Jessop, Wayland Publishers Ltd (Unit 28)

New Caribbean Junior Reader 2, Ginn & Company (Unit 29)

Computers for Beginners, Margaret Shepherd and Rebecca Treays, Usborne Publishing Ltd (Unit 33)

The following items were written especially for Key Comprehension Book 2
Page from *Maths Dictionary* (Unit 31)

"Church choir" and "There was a young lady" (Unit 34)

Dear Householder (Unit 35)

Record keeping

The following record keeping sheets are provided for the teacher's convenience.

Class record sheet

The record sheet on page 16 gives an overall picture of the marks gained in each Unit by every pupil in the class.

Pupil record sheet

The record sheet on page 17 can be used to record in detail each pupil's performance in reading comprehension.

The questions set in each Unit are arranged to highlight the type of reading comprehension tested. Question numbers appear in the top part of each rectangle leaving space in the lower part to indicate that each question has been attempted by the pupil.

The right-hand column provides space to record the total mark out of 15 gained in each Unit.

READING COMPREHENSION: Class record sheet

CLASS: YEAR: TEACHER:

PUPILS' NAMES	1	2	3	4	5	6	7	8	9	10	11	12	13	14	15	16	17	18	19	20	21	22	23	24	25	26	27	28	29	30	31	32	33	34	35	36	37

UNITS (EACH MARKED OUT OF 15)

READING COMPREHENSION: Pupil record sheet

NAME:	CLASS:	YEAR:

UNIT	LITERAL	DEDUCTIVE	INFERENTIAL	EVAL.	COMMENTS	MARK	DATE
1	1 2 3 4 5						
2			1 2 3 4				
3	4 8		2 5 9				
4	3 4	1	2 5 6				
5	4 6	1 7 8 9 10	2 3 5				
6	1		2 3 4 5				
7	1 2 3 4 5 6 7						
8	6		3 4 8 10				
9			1 2 3 4 5				
10	4 5 6	2	1 3	7			
11	2 4	6	1 3 5	7			
12			1 2 3 4 5				
13	1 3 4 5	6	2				
14	1 2 3 4 6 8 10	7 9	5				
15	1 2 5	6 7	3 4				
16	1 2	4	3 5				
17		1 5	2 3 4	6			
18	1 2 3 4 7	10	5 6 8 9				
19	1 2 4 6 8	3 5 7		9			
20	3	2 5 6 7	1 4				
21	1 2 3 4 5 6 7 8 9 10 11 12						
22	1 2	3 5 6 7	4				
23	1 3	5	2 4				
24	1 4 6 10 13						
25	1 3	5	2 4 6				
26	1	3 5 6 7 8	2 4				
27	1 2 4 7 9	8	3 5 6 10				
28	1 2 3 4 5	6 7					
29	1 5 7 8 12						
30	1 2 6	7 10	3 4 5	8 9			
31	6	1 2 4 7 8 9 10	3 5				
32		2 3	1 4 5 6 7 8 9				
33	2 5	1 3 4 6 7					
34	1 2 6 8	3 4	5	7			
35	1 4 5 6 8	7 9 10	2 3 11				
36	5a 7a	4	1 2 3 6	5b 7b			
37	3 5 7 10	9 11	1 2 4 8	6			

PART TWO

Answers, mark scheme and extension activities

Answers follow for each Unit of Key Comprehension Book 2, together with a suggested mark scheme and suggestions for extension activities. Teachers may wish to photocopy relevant pages to allow pupils to mark their own work from the answers provided and to work on the Extension Activities suggested.

Answers

The activities often remind pupils to answer in full sentences in order to develop good practice from the outset. The answers suggested in the Teachers' Handbook are therefore supplied in full sentences where appropriate. In some places, open-ended questions invite a variety of possible answers and where this is the case, guidance is given on the kinds of response that are acceptable.

Mark scheme

The suggested mark scheme marks each Unit out of 15 to allow for some flexibility of response. Teachers may choose to award the suggested marks for accuracy of reading comprehension alone; or they may wish to reserve a part of each allocated mark for spelling, punctuation and sentence construction (for example, whether answers are written in full sentences). Pupils benefit from being fully involved in the assessment of their work. Therefore, any chosen criteria for marking should be shared with them. Towards this aim, the suggested number of marks for each question in each Unit is given in the Pupil Book. A photocopiable whole class record sheet is provided on page 16 and an individual pupil record sheet on page 17.

Extension activities

The extension activities offer opportunities for further work in reading comprehension, language work and writing in a wide range of genres. The specific skills covered are summarised at the end of each set of extension activities.

Walpole

UNIT 1

GENRE	fiction: animal
READING STRATEGIES	skimming; scanning; detailed reading
QUESTION FORM	cloze
UNDERSTANDING TESTED	all questions – literal
CURRICULUM LINK	science; PSHE

1 Why did the oldest walrus want Walpole to be the leader?
   He wanted Walpole to be the leader because Walpole was the <u>biggest</u> and the
   <u>strongest</u> walrus in the herd.   *(3 marks)*

2 What did Walpole want to do instead of being the leader?
   Walpole wanted to look after <u>the baby walruses</u> who had lost their <u>mothers</u>.   *(3 marks)*

3 What did the baby walruses love to see Walpole doing?
   They loved to see him walk on his <u>flippers</u> and <u>shake</u> all over.   *(3 marks)*

4 What kind of things did Walpole do for the little walruses?
   He gave them <u>rides</u> on his back.
   He found <u>food</u> for them.
   He made sure that they didn't <u>float</u> away on a piece of <u>ice</u>.   *(3 marks)*

5 What animals would never hurt the walruses if Walpole was there?
   The <u>polar bears</u> would never hurt the walruses if Walpole was there.   *(3 marks)*

Extension activities

1 The walruses sometimes pushed each other out of the way to get the best place
   on the rocks but they never tried to push Walpole. Why?

2 What sound did the baby walruses make when they were excited?

3 What is the word for a large group of walruses living together?

4 What are tusks?

5 Do you think Walpole should have agreed to be the leader? Why?

6 Pretend you are one of the baby walruses. Explain how you feel about Walpole
   and why.

7 Find out more words for groups of things. (We call these "collective nouns".)

   a) a s _ _ _ _ of bees   f) a b _ _ _ _ of flowers

   b) a f _ _ _ _ of sheep   g) a s _ _ _ _ of fish

   c) a p _ _ _ of wolves   h) a h _ _ _ of cows

   d) a f _ _ _ _ of ships   i) a s _ _ _ _ _ of whales

   e) a h _ _ _ of angels   j) a r _ _ _ _ _ _ _ of soldiers

SPECIFIC SKILLS	additional comprehension questions; writing in character; language work (collective nouns)

Making a moving cat

GENRE	instructions
READING STRATEGIES	skimming; scanning; detailed reading
QUESTION FORM	sequencing
UNDERSTANDING TESTED	all questions – inferential
CURRICULUM LINK	design and technology

The sentences should be sequenced in this order:

1 *First, draw the shape of a cat's head and body on card and cut it out.*

2 *Draw two legs and a tail, making sure they are at least 2 cm wide. The legs should be about 10 cm long and the tail about 25 cm long.*

3 *Fix the legs only to the back of the cat's body with paper fasteners. Fix the tail to the top of the legs, but not to the body, with fasteners. Now you can move the tail and the legs will also move.*

4 *Finally, paint the cat's face and body on the other side of the card.*

(3 marks for each instruction in correct position + 3 marks for spelling, punctuation and handwriting)

Extension activities

1 Think of something you know how to make out of paper, such as a paper aeroplane or a fortune-teller. Write clear instructions with diagrams to explain how to make the thing you have chosen.

2 Imagine that you have made a moving cat and a moving mouse and you are going to use them to put on a puppet show. Write the conversation that the cat and the mouse would have in your show.

3 Think of a hobby that you enjoy which involves making things, such as playing with building bricks, making models, making birthday cards or making cakes or sweets. Write about your hobby and what you make. Use the sentence beginnings below to help you.

Something that I enjoy doing is...

There are several reasons why I enjoy this hobby. The first reason is that...

Another reason is that...

The best thing about my hobby is that...

Usually I make things like...

Sometimes it is quite difficult because...

The best thing that I ever made was...

SPECIFIC SKILLS	writing instructions; writing imaginative dialogue; autobiographical writing

How to feed your rabbit

GENRE	instructions
READING STRATEGIES	skimming; scanning; detailed reading
QUESTION FORM	true/false
UNDERSTANDING TESTED	questions 4, 8 – literal; 2, 5, 9 – inferential
CURRICULUM LINK	science; PSHE

The true statements are:

2 *Rabbits' teeth go on growing.*   (3 marks)

4 *You should try to feed your rabbit at the same times every day.*   (3 marks)

5 *Rabbits have sharp teeth.*   (3 marks)

8 *Pet rabbits should be given wood to bite and chew.*   (3 marks)

9 *A rabbit's food bowl needs to be quite heavy.*   (3 marks)

Extension activities

1 Give two reasons why a plastic food bowl is unsuitable for a rabbit.

2 Why do you think it is safer and cleaner to use a water bottle with a spout rather than an ordinary bowl?

3 What is meant by "a regular feeding routine"?

4 Silent letters: **g**

   The word **gnaw** was used in the passage. Gnaw begins with a silent **g**. Complete these other silent **g** words.

   a) a small stinging insect **g** _ _ _
   b) a kind of fairy who lives underground **g** _ _ _ _
   c) grind your teeth together in anger **g** _ _ _ _

5 Silent letters: **k**

   Complete these silent **k** words.

   a) a joint in the middle of the leg: **k** _ _ _
   b) a tool with a sharp blade used for cutting: **k** _ _ _ _
   c) a joint in the finger: **k** _ _ _ _ _ _

6 Use books in your class library to find out what food you should give to a pet rabbit to make sure it stays healthy. Make a list of the foods you should give.

7 Imagine that you are going on holiday and a friend is going to look after your pet. Write a list of all the things your friend needs to do.

SPECIFIC SKILLS	additional comprehension questions; silent g and silent k; research and retrieval; listing instructions

Disappearing water

GENRE	instructions/explanation
READING STRATEGIES	skimming; scanning; detailed reading
QUESTION FORMS	cloze; sentence completion
UNDERSTANDING TESTED	question 1 – deductive; 2, 5, 6 – inferential; 3, 4 – literal
CURRICULUM LINK	science

1 What do you do to wet things when you wring them out?
You take them in your hands and you <u>twist them until all the water comes out</u>. (3 marks)

2 Which of the cloths was drier the next day?
The cloth that was <u>spread on the plate</u> was drier the next day. (3 marks)

3 Where does water go when it evaporates?
When water evaporates, it goes <u>into the air</u>. (2 marks)

4 How long does the rainbow sugar mixture take to dry out?
It takes <u>three days</u> to dry out. (2 marks)

5 Is it safe to eat the sugar when it is ready?
It is <u>safe</u> to eat the sugar. (2 marks)

6 Why is the sugar called "rainbow sugar"?
It is called "rainbow sugar" because <u>it is a mixture of different colours</u>. (3 marks)

Extension activities

1 Why did the cloth in the plastic bag stay wet?

2 Why do you think it is a good idea to put the two cloths in a warm place?

3 "Disappear" is the opposite of "appear". The word is made by adding "**dis-**" to the front. Change the following words to make their opposite meaning by adding one of the following prefixes.

dis-   un-   im-

a) patient	f) helpful	k) cover
b) happy	g) usual	l) satisfied
c) organised	h) perfect	m) pleased
d) practical	i) pure	n) sure
e) dressed	j) agree	o) possible

SPECIFIC SKILLS   additional comprehension questions; prefixes

---

U N I T 5

Luke's pet spider

GENRE	fiction: realistic; familiar setting
READING STRATEGIES	skimming; scanning; detailed reading
QUESTION FORMS	multiple choice
UNDERSTANDING TESTED	questions 1, 7, 8, 9, 10 – deductive; 2, 3, 5 – inferential; 4, 6 – literal
CURRICULUM LINK	science; PSHE

1 Who was Luke talking to at the beginning of the passage?
   c) Luke was talking to his teacher and everyone in the class.   (1.5 marks)

2 Why did Mrs Matthews say, "Is that all, Luke?" when he sat down?
   c) She didn't think he had said enough.   (1.5 marks)

3 How long had Luke had his pet spider?
   a) Luke had had the spider for a few hours.   (1.5 marks)

4 How did Luke get his spider?
   b) Luke's mother found the spider under his bed.   (1.5 marks)

5 Why wouldn't the lady who lived downstairs let Luke have a pet?
   c) She didn't want to upset her dog.   (1.5 marks)

6 Why didn't Luke write about his neighbour's pet?
   c) He didn't want to.   (1.5 marks)

7 Why did Luke shut the shoebox lid quickly when he started to show
   his spider to the class?
   a) He thought the spider might escape.   (1.5 marks)

8 Why did Mrs Matthews shudder when she saw the spider's legs?
   b) She was frightened of spiders.   (1.5 marks)

9 What does "dangled" mean?
   c) "Dangled" means "hung loosely".   (1.5 marks)

10 What is the plural of box?
   c) "Boxes" is the plural of "box".   (1.5 marks)

Extension activities

1 Do you think a spider would make a good pet? Why?

2 Mrs Matthews was frightened of spiders. She could not help it. Are you
   frightened of anything that can't really hurt you? Write about how you feel.

3 Pretend you are Dizzy the spider. Describe your day from the moment that
   Luke's mother found you under the bed.

SPECIFIC SKILLS	Expressing and justifying an opinion; personal writing; writing in character

I am better than you

GENRE	fiction: animal
READING STRATEGIES	skimming; scanning; detailed reading (and conventions of layout of dialogue)
QUESTION FORMS	questions requiring answers in complete sentences; multiple choice; true/false
UNDERSTANDING TESTED	question 1 – literal; questions 2, 3, 4, 5 – inferential
CURRICULUM LINK	science

1 Why did Sam think he was better than Pete?
Either: *Sam thought he was prettier than Pete.*
Or: *Sam thought he could do things that Pete could not do.* *(3 marks)*

2 What could Pete do just as well as Sam?
Pete could catch a fly just as well as Sam. *(3 marks)*

3 Which of the following words describes Sam best?
friendly   boastful   hungry
"Boastful" describes Sam best. *(3 marks)*

4 Is it true that Pete believed everything that Sam said?
No, it is false. *(3 marks)*

5 Write down three words from the passage that rhyme with "fly".
Three words from the passage that rhyme with "fly" are: my, I, why. *(3 marks)*

Extension activities

1 Sam and Pete are lizards. If they were two boys, what kind of things might they say?

2 The five sentences below are taken from the passage. Three of the sentences need a full stop at the end, one needs a question mark and one needs an exclamation mark. Write out the sentences with the correct punctuation mark at the end. When you have finished, look back at the passage to see if you are right.

   a) One day on a vine, a lizard named Sam met a lizard named Pete
   b) Get out of my way
   c) Why are you the best lizard there is
   d) I can do things that you cannot do
   e) Pete got a fly too

3 Look carefully at how the inverted commas (" ") are used to show what Sam and Pete said to each other. Then add the inverted commas where they are needed in the following sentences.

   a) What is the time? asked Amelia.
   b) Stop talking! snapped Mrs Brown.
   c) I am so hungry, whispered Kathleen.
   d) Yes, said John. So am I.

SPECIFIC SKILLS	Rewriting a conversation for different context; practice in using end stops and inverted commas

The smallest bird in the world and the largest bird in the world

GENRE	information: report
READING STRATEGIES	skimming; scanning; detailed reading
QUESTION FORM	questions requiring answers in complete sentences
UNDERSTANDING TESTED	all questions – literal
CURRICULUM LINK	science

1 What part of a humming bird makes a humming noise?
   The wings of a humming bird make a humming noise.   *(1 mark)*

2 What do ostriches use their wings for?
   Ostriches use their wings to help them keep their balance when they run fast.   *(2 marks)*

3 Write down two ways in which a humming bird is like a helicopter.
   *Like a helicopter a humming bird can hover/stay in one place in the air and like
   a helicopter, a humming bird can fly backwards.*   *(2 + 2 marks)*

4 Write down two ways in which an ostrich is like a horse.
   An ostrich can run as fast as a horse and it can kick as hard as a horse.   *(2 + 2 marks)*

5 Why are the smallest kind of humming birds called bee humming birds?
   They are called bee humming birds because they are almost as small as a bee.   *(2 marks)*

6 In which country would you see bee humming birds flying around?
   You would see bee humming birds in Cuba.   *(1 mark)*

7 Where do most ostriches live?
   Most ostriches live in Africa.   *(1 mark)*

Extension activities

1 Read the passage again and complete these sentences.

   a) The humming bird is just like _____
   b) Most other birds are like _____
   c) An ostrich is as tall as _____
   d) It can run as fast as _____

3 Similes

   All the comparisons in the last exercise are similes.

   Think of good similes to complete these sentences.

   a) The little kitten was as warm as _____.
   b) The baby's cheek was as soft as _____.
   c) The children were as quiet as _____ .
   d) David looked as white as a _____.

SPECIFIC SKILLS	similes

Sally

GENRE	fiction: realistic
READING STRATEGIES	skimming; scanning; detailed reading
QUESTION FORM	true/false
UNDERSTANDING TESTED	questions 3, 4, 8, 10 – inferential; 6 – literal
CURRICULUM LINK	music

The true statements are:

3 *Sally closed the door whenever Peter asked.*   *(3 marks)*

4 *Sally talked by growling whenever Peter asked.*   *(3 marks)*

6 *Sally made a terrible noise when she put her paws on the piano keyboard.*   *(3 marks)*

8 *Sally was a black-and-white collie dog.*   *(3 marks)*

10 *Peter thought Sally was very intelligent.*   *(3 marks)*

Extension activities

1 What do the following words from the passage mean?

    a) alert   d) growled
    b) intelligent   e) slammed
    c) silent   f) discord

2 Peter thought it would be "a piece of cake" for Sally to play the piano. What did he mean by "a piece of cake"?

3 How did Peter get Sally to put her paws on the keyboard?

4 List six tricks that Sally could do.

5 How can you tell that Sally and Peter were good friends?

6 Look at the pictures of Peter and his mother.

    a) How do you think Peter felt when Sally put her paws on the keyboard?
    b) How do you think Peter's mother felt?

7 Write a letter from Peter to his Aunt Win telling her about all about the tricks that Sally can do.

8 Write about a pet you know who can do clever things. Include the following details:

    what sort of animal it is
    what its name is
    whose pet it is
    what tricks it can do
    how it learned to do its tricks

SPECIFIC SKILLS	comprehension questions; descriptive writing; letter writing; summaries

Making nettle paper

GENRE	instructions
READING STRATEGIES	skimming; scanning; detailed reading
QUESTION FORM	sequencing
UNDERSTANDING TESTED	all questions – inferential
CURRICULUM LINK	science; art; design and technology

The sentences should be sequenced in this order:

1 *Put on the gardening gloves and pull about 50 leaves off some stinging nettle plants.*

2 *Keeping your gloves on, cut the stinging nettle leaves into small pieces and soak them in a bucket of cold water for two or three days.*

3 *Drain the water out of the bucket and ask a grown-up to boil the leaves in a saucepan half-full of water until they turn a pale yellow colour. Leave them in the saucepan until the water is cool.*

4 *Scoop the leaves out of the saucepan with a sieve and spread them out carefully on some newspaper on a flat surface. The fibres of the nettle leaves will bind together as they dry to make a sheet of thick yellowy "paper".*

5 *Cover the damp "paper" with more newspapers and press with two or three heavy books.*

6 *Remove your handmade sheet of paper after two days.*

(2.5 marks for each instruction correctly positioned)

Extension activities

1 Why is it important to wear gloves when you make nettle paper?

2 How long do you have to soak the leaves in a bucket of water?

3 How long must the leaves be boiled for?

4 What do you do after you have boiled the leaves?

5 How do you get the leaves out of the saucepan?

6 How long do you have to press the damp paper for?

7 What colour is the finished paper?

8 What do the following words mean?

   a) drain   e) sieve

   b) boil   f) fibres

   c) soak   g) handmade

   d) sting   h) bind

SPECIFIC SKILLS	comprehension questions; vocabulary

Dragon breath

GENRE	fiction: fantasy
READING STRATEGIES	skimming; scanning; detailed reading
QUESTION FORM	questions requiring answers in complete sentences
UNDERSTANDING TESTED	questions 1, 3 – inferential, 2 – deductive; 4, 5, 6 – literal; 7 – evaluative
CURRICULUM LINK	English

1 Why was Snap unhappy?
He was unhappy because he couldn't breathe fire (like other dragons).   *(2 marks)*

2 "Snap shuffled into the kitchen." How do you walk if you shuffle?
When you shuffle, you drag your feet along the ground.   *(2 marks)*

3 What two things do you learn about Vera that make you think she liked to be fit and healthy?
Vera had been out jogging in the forest (as she did every day) and she was drinking carrot juice (which is good for you).   *(1 + 1 marks)*

4 Why did Snap want to breathe fire?
*He wanted to breathe fire because that is what dragons do.
(He wanted to be like other dragons.)*   *(1 mark)*

5 What two signs always showed that Snap was going to cry?
The two signs were: sticking out his bottom lip and starting to sniff to himself.   *(1 + 1 marks)*

6 Why did Vera not want Snap to cry?
She didn't want him to cry because his tears stained the carpet.   *(2 marks)*

7 If you were Vera, what would you say to cheer Snap up?
*Open. Reward any sensible answers. Vera is sensible, practical and motherly.
She is likely to tell him that she likes him just as he is; that breathing fire will come in good time; that if he cries he will never be able to breathe fire etc.)*   *(4 marks)*

Extension activities

1 Pretend you are Vera. You keep a diary and write about ten sentences in it every day. Today you are writing about Snap being unhappy. What would you write?

2 Write a story about a dragon who can breathe fire who helps someone by breathing fire at the right time.

3 Snap is unhappy because he can't breathe fire. Have you ever been unhappy because you couldn't do something you wanted to be able to do? Write about what happened and how you felt.

SPECIFIC SKILLS	writing a diary entry in character; writing a narrative; autobiographical writing

Mrs Goat and her seven kids

GENRE	traditional tale
READING STRATEGIES	skimming; scanning; detailed reading
QUESTION FORM	questions requiring answers in complete sentences
UNDERSTANDING TESTED	questions 1, 3, 5 – inferential; 2, 4, – literal; 6 – deductive; 7 – evaluative
CURRICULUM LINK	PSHE

1 Which word in the passage means "young goats"?
   The word "kids" means "young goats".   (2 marks)

2 Why couldn't the goats open the door to anyone while their mother was out?
   They couldn't open the door because the Hungry Wolf might get in and eat them. (2 marks)

3 How did the Hungry Wolf try to trick them into opening the door the first time
   he knocked?
   He pretended he was their mother and said he wanted to give them pocket money. (2 marks)

4 How did the little goats know he was not their mother?
   They knew he was not their mother because he hadn't got her squeaky voice. (2 marks)

5 How did the Hungry Wolf try to trick them the second time?
   *The second time, he tried to speak in a squeaky voice and said he had some
   sweets for them.*   (2 marks)

6 How do you think the little goats will know he is not their mother this time?
   *They will know when he puts his paw through the letterbox because it won't look
   like their mother's hoof.*   (2 marks)

7 Think of three words that would describe the smallest and youngest goat.
   He seems to have a lot to say!
   Accept any three sensible suggestions.
   Answers might include: lively, talkative, boastful, clever, sensible, brave, (3 marks)
   shrewd, obedient.

Extension activities

1 Continue the story. Think of one more trick the wolf might play on the little
   goats. Say whether the trick works or not.

2 A young goat is called a "kid". What do we call the following young animals?

   a) a young fox   c _ _   f) a young duck   d _ _ _ _ _ _ _
   b) a young deer   f _ _ _   g) a young horse   f _ _ _
   c) a young swan   c _ _ _ _ _   h) a young wolf   c _ _
   d) a young hare   l _ _ _ _ _ _ i) a young cow   c _ _ _
   e) a young goose   g _ _ _ _ _ _ j) a young sheep   l _ _ _

SPECIFIC SKILLS	extending the story; vocabulary

GENRE	information: report
READING STRATEGIES	skimming; scanning; detailed reading
QUESTION FORM	questions requiring answers in complete sentences
UNDERSTANDING TESTED	all questions – inferential
CURRICULUM LINK	science

1 What do grey herons eat?
Grey herons eat fish and water animals.   (3 marks)

2 What do reed warblers eat?
Reed warblers eat insects.   (3 marks)

3 What do hawfinches eat?
Hawfinches eat seeds and nuts.   (3 marks)

4 What do mallard eat?
Mallard eat tiny water plants and water animals.   (3 marks)

5 Is a tawny owl a meat eater, a seed eater, a fish eater or a plant eater?
A tawny owl is a meat eater.   (3 marks)

Extension activities

1 Choose one of the birds and find out more about it. Use books in your class library to help you. Write an account of what you find out.

Find out about the following things:

What does it look like?
Which country does it live in?
What habitat does it like?
Where does it build its nest?
What do its eggs look like?
How many eggs does it lay?
What are its chicks like?
Does it migrate? If so, where does it go?

2 An animal or human skull with a full set of teeth would show some interesting things about the eating habits of the creature. Find out how the following differently shaped teeth are used to chew food:

a) molars
b) incisors
c) canines

SPECIFIC SKILLS	research and retrieval; writing an account

Mrs Cockle

GENRE	fiction: significant author
READING STRATEGIES	skimming; scanning; detailed reading
QUESTION FORM	questions requiring answers in complete sentences
UNDERSTANDING TESTED	questions 1, 3, 4, 5 – literal; 2 – inferential; 6 – deductive
CURRICULUM LINK	PSHE

1 How did Mrs Cockle feel about having to climb so many stairs?
She didn't mind having to climb so many stairs. (2 marks)

2 Why did Mrs Cockle like living at the top of the house?
Give as many reasons as you can.
She had a good view from the top of the house. She could see the sky over the tall house opposite. She could see what the weather was going to be like so she could decide what to wear. (3 marks)

3 Why did Mrs Cockle need three umbrellas?
She had a different umbrella for each different kind of weather. (2 marks)

4 What did Mrs Cockle wear when the sky was blue?
She wore her straw bonnet. (2 marks)

5 What did Mrs Cockle wear when the sky was white?
She wore her shawl. (2 marks)

6 What do the following words mean?
a) *"Advantage" means something that is lucky or fortunate or worthwhile.* (1 mark)
b) *"Bonnet" means a type of hat that fastens under the chin.* (1 mark)
c) *"Shawl" means a triangle or square of cloth worn over the shoulders.* (1 mark)
d) *"Trapdoor" means a flat door in a roof or a floor.* (1 mark)

Extension activities

1 Write a sentence for each of the following words.

a) wear   where
b) right   write
c) made   maid
d) more   moor

2 Imagine you go to see Mrs Cockle. Describe your visit.

3 Look at the picture of Mrs Cockle climbing out on to her roof. Write a conversation with her where you are telling her how dangerous it is.

4 There are advantages and disadvantages in living at the top of the house for Mrs Cockle. What are the advantages and disadvantages of living where you live?

5 Describe an interesting old person you know. Write about all the unusual and special things about him or her.

SPECIFIC SKILLS	homophones; story extension; writing a conversation; reflective writing; describing a person

Children's library guide

GENRE	information: leaflet
READING STRATEGIES	skimming; scanning; detailed reading
QUESTION FORM	multiple choice
UNDERSTANDING TESTED	questions 1, 2, 3, 4, 6, 8, 10 – literal; 7, 9 – deductive; 5 – inferential
CURRICULUM LINK	English

1 Who should sign the form when you join the library?
   b) *A parent should sign the form when you join the library.*   (1.5 marks)

2 How much does it cost to join the library?
   c) *It costs nothing to join the library.*   (1.5 marks)

3 How many books can you borrow at a time from this library?
   a) *You can borrow eight books at a time from this library.*   (1.5 marks)

4 How long can you keep the books for?
   b) *You can keep the books for four weeks.*   (1.5 marks)

5 Can someone who is three years old join this library?
   b) Yes, someone who is three can join this library.   (1.5 marks)

6 What can you borrow as well as books?
   a) *You can borrow cassettes.*   (1.5 marks)

7 Which writer comes nearest the beginning of the story section?
   a) *Roald Dahl comes nearest the beginning of the story section.*   (1.5 marks)

8 What happens if you don't return your books on time?
   a) *You have to pay some money to the library.*   (1.5 marks)

9 Which word means: "arrange for a book to be kept especially for you"?
   c) *"Reserve" means "arrange for a book to be kept especially for you".*   (1.5 marks)

10 What is the plural of "library"?
   c) *The plural of "library" is "libraries".*   (1.5 marks)

Extension activities

1 Use your class library to find the title of one book by each of the following authors:

   a) Anne Fine   b) Gene Kemp   c) Roald Dahl

2 Write a book review about a book that you have enjoyed reading. Include the following information:
   – the title and author of the book
   – what the book was about
   – what you thought was the best part
   – anything you didn't like about the book
   – why you enjoyed the book so much

SPECIFIC SKILLS	research and retrieval; writing a book review

Bicycle safety

GENRE	information: report
READING STRATEGIES	skimming; scanning; detailed reading
QUESTION FORM	questions requiring answers in complete sentences
UNDERSTANDING TESTED	questions 1, 2, 5 – literal; 3, 4 – inferential; 6, 7 – deductive
CURRICULUM LINK	PE; PSHE

1 Why is it sensible for people to wear brightly coloured clothes when they are riding a bicycle in traffic?
It is sensible for people to wear brightly coloured clothes so that they can be seen easily by other road users. (2 marks)

2 Why should cyclists wear a safety helmet?
Cyclists should wear a safety helmet to protect themselves against head injuries if they fall off their bicycle. Head injuries can be very severe. (2 marks)

3 Would it be good advice or bad advice if someone told you to oil your bicycle every day? Why?
It would be bad advice. You would be oiling your bicycle too much and you would risk getting grit and dust stuck to the oil. This would soon damage your bicycle. (1 + 1 marks)

4 Give three reasons why it is a good idea to pass your cycling proficiency test before you ride a bicycle in traffic. Reward any three:
Cyclists who have passed the test will know the rules of the road; will understand signals; will understand road signs; will know when they have to use lights; will keep their bicycles in good working order (brakes etc.); will know how to ride their bicycles safely (getting on and off etc.); will know about safety helmets; will know about bright clothes being a safety factor. (2 + 2 + 2 marks)

5 Which bicycle light is red, the front or the back light?
The back light is red. (1 mark)

6 Which word in the passage means "keeping in good working order"?
The word "maintenance" means "keeping in good working order". (1 mark)

7 What word could you use instead of "lubricated" in the following sentence?
"The chain should be cleaned and lubricated."
"Oiled" could be used instead of "lubricated". (1 mark)

Extension activities

1 It is very important to wear a safety helmet when you are cycling. Make a poster that gets this message across.

2 If you have a bicycle, describe it and any accessories you have for it.

3 Do you think car drivers and motor cyclists are considerate enough to cyclists? What advice would you give them?

4 Find out and write down details about the next cycling proficiency test in your area.

SPECIFIC SKILLS	making a poster; writing a descriptive account; research and retrieval

UNIT 16

Beware, Princess!

GENRE	fiction: modern fairy tale
READING STRATEGIES	skimming; scanning; detailed reading
QUESTION FORM	questions requiring answers in complete sentences
UNDERSTANDING TESTED	questions 1, 2 – literal; 4 – deductive; 3, 5 – inferential
CURRICULUM LINK	English

1 What colour were Poppy's eyes?
Poppy's eyes were brown. *(2 marks)*

2 Did Poppy have long hair or short hair?
Poppy had short hair. *(2 marks)*

3 Why did Poppy's dresses get so torn and dirty?
They got torn and dirty because she played outside a lot. *(2 marks)*

4 What do the following words and phrases mean?
a) *"Advantage" means something that is lucky or fortunate or worthwhile.* *(1 mark)*
b) *"Heir to the throne" means a person who will be the next king or queen.* *(1 mark)*
c) *"Beat about the bush" means not saying what you mean.* *(1 mark)*
d) *"Interrupt" means talk over someone else while they are speaking.* *(1 mark)*
e) *"Ogre" means a fierce giant.* *(1 mark)*
f) *"Innocent" means being ignorant about bad things.* *(1 mark)*

5 The passage comes from a story called "Beware, Princess!" Why do you think it is called that?
Reward any sensible answer that suggests the title is a warning that Poppy will have to be very careful because there is an ogre who wants to eat her. *(3 marks)*

Extension activities

1 Why do you think a girl like Poppy is a great favourite with the castle guards, the cook and the gardener?

2 Explain why Poppy's parents are "perhaps a little disappointed" by her.

3 The ogre is described as having rather "traditional" tastes. What does "traditional" mean?

4 Give one adjective to describe the King and one adjective to describe the Queen.

5 How do you think Poppy feels at the end of the passage?

6 Poppy had a "really royal tea" on her ninth birthday. What do you think she had to eat and drink at her birthday tea? Write a vivid and mouth-watering description.

7 It was Poppy's <u>ninth</u> birthday.
Can you spell the words for the following numbers?
1st, 2nd, 3rd, 4th, 5th, 6th, 7th, 8th, 10th, 11th, 12th, 13th, 14th, 15th

SPECIFIC SKILLS	additional comprehension questions; descriptive writing; spelling

The lion and his three counsellors

GENRE	fable
READING STRATEGIES	skimming; scanning; detailed reading
QUESTION FORM	questions requiring answers in complete sentences
UNDERSTANDING TESTED	questions 1, 5 – deductive; 2, 3, 4 – inferential; 6 – evaluative
CURRICULUM LINK	PSHE; English

1 What was the actual question that the lion asked the sheep?
The lion asked the sheep, "Does <u>my breath smell?</u>" (2 marks)

2 In what way was the sheep foolish?
The sheep was foolish to tell the wolf the truth when he didn't want to hear that answer. (2 marks)

3 Why did the lion kill the wolf?
The lion killed the wolf because he didn't believe him. (2 marks)

4 Explain how the fox was being very clever when he said he had a cold.
The fox gave a good excuse for not being able to answer the question, so he couldn't give the wrong answer and make the lion angry again. (3 marks)

5 What do the following words mean?
 a) *"Flatterer" means someone who says kind things which are not true just to please someone.* (1 mark)
 b) *"Crafty" means sly or cunning.* (1 mark)
 c) *"Finally" means at last.* (1 mark)

6 Explain the moral of the story in your own words.
"Wise men keep a guard on their tongues" means <u>sensible people are careful about what they say</u>. (3 marks)

Extension activities

1 What is another word for "replied"?

2 Explain in your own words, "He fared no better".

3 The lion asked the fox "his opinion on the matter". This means that the lion asked the fox what he _____.

4 Think about whether you have ever had to be careful about what you said when someone asked your opinion. Would you say that you are more like the sheep, the wolf or the fox in the story?

5 This story is a fable by Aesop. A fable is a special kind of story with a moral. Find some other fables by Aesop in your class library and retell one of the stories in your own words.

6 Write a fable of your own with the moral: "It is always better to tell the truth".

SPECIFIC SKILLS	comprehension; reflective writing; retelling a story; writing a fable

Uninvited ghosts

GENRE	fiction: fantasy; significant author
READING STRATEGIES	skimming; scanning; detailed reading
QUESTION FORM	questions requiring answers in complete sentences
UNDERSTANDING TESTED	questions 1, 2, 3, 4, 7 – literal; 10 – deductive; 5, 6, 8, 9 – inferential
CURRICULUM LINK	English

1   What did the Browns lose in the move?
    They lost their kettle.   (1 mark)

2   What was broken?
    Mrs Brown's favourite vase was broken.   (1 mark)

3   What did the Brown family have for supper?
    They had bread and baked beans for supper.   (1 mark)

4   What did the cat do that made people cross?
    The cat was sick on the sitting-room carpet.   (1 mark)

5   Why did Mr and Mrs Brown send Marian and Simon to bed early?
    Their parents had probably had enough and wanted some peace and quiet.   (1.5 marks)

6   How did Marian and Simon feel when they were sent to bed early?
    They didn't really mind.   (1.5 marks)

7   The ghost was not very frightening but it was very annoying.
    Write down two annoying things that it did.
    *Any two from: it made humming noises; it made clacking noises when it was
    knitting; it told the children off like an adult; it argued; it wouldn't go away.*   (1 + 1 marks)

8   Why didn't Mrs Brown believe the children when they told her about the ghost?
    *She didn't believe them and thought they were making it all up because she couldn't
    see or hear the ghost.*   (2 marks)

9   How do we know that the Browns moved into a house that is at least one
    hundred years old?
    *We know the house is at least one hundred years old because the ghost has been
    in the house for longer than that.*   (2 marks)

10 Which word tells us that Marian was really miserable when she saw two ghosts
    in the bedroom on the second night?
    The word "wailed" tells us that Marian was miserable.   (2 marks)

Extension activities

1   Write the conversation that the children had with Mrs Brown when she came up to
    their bedroom and they told her about the ghost that she couldn't see.

2   Write about the sort of house that you would like to live in. Write about what it
    would look like, where it would be, what rooms it would have, how you would use
    each room and what the garden would be like.

SPECIFIC SKILLS	writing a conversation; personal writing; imaginative writing

The magic finger

GENRE	fiction: fantasy; significant author
READING STRATEGIES	skimming; scanning; detailed reading
QUESTION FORM	questions requiring answers in complete sentences
UNDERSTANDING TESTED	questions 1, 2, 4, 6, 8 – literal; 3, 5, 7 – deductive; 9 – evaluative
CURRICULUM LINK	PSHE citizenship

1 Which of Mr Gregg's sons was the same age as the girl who is telling the story?
Philip was the same age. *(1 mark)*

2 What job did Mr Gregg do?
Mr Gregg was a farmer. *(2 marks)*

3 How do you know that the girl and the two boys were friends?
We know they were friends because sometimes the girl went to play with them. *(2 marks)*

4 What did Mr Gregg and his sons love doing every Saturday morning?
They loved hunting and shooting animals in the wood. *(1 mark)*

5 The girl didn't like what Mr Gregg and his sons did so she tried to "talk them out of it". What does "talk them out of it" mean?
It means she tried to persuade them not to do it. *(2 marks)*

6 How did the girl feel when she saw they had killed a young deer?
It made her feel very angry. *(2 marks)*

7 How do we know that the boys weren't at all sorry for what they had done?
We know they weren't sorry because they just laughed. *(2 marks)*

8 What strange thing did the girl say she did to the Greggs before she could stop herself?
She said that she put the magic finger on them. *(1 mark)*

9 This passage comes from the opening of a book. Do you think it would make people want to read the rest of the book to find out what happens next? Why?
Reward any sensible well-supported answer whether positive or negative. *(2 marks)*

Extension activities

1 What is your opinion about hunting? Explain your answer.

2 When the girl was angry, she says she "saw red". Complete the following sayings with the correct colours.

   a) The poor child was _____ with cold.
   b) Every cloud has a _____ lining.
   c) We were _____ with envy when we saw her prize.
   d) The baby was as good as _____.
   e) James was as _____ as a sheet when he heard the news.
   f) After I'd fallen off the horse I was _____ and _____ all over.

SPECIFIC SKILLS	expressing an opinion; metaphors and similes

Life's not been the same in my family

GENRE	poem: significant poet
READING STRATEGIES	skimming; scanning; detailed reading
QUESTION FORM	multiple choice
UNDERSTANDING TESTED	question 3 – literal; 2, 5, 6, 7 – deductive; 1, 4 – inferential
CURRICULUM LINK	PSHE; science

1 How did the girl feel about the new baby in her family?
   a) The girl was jealous of the new baby.   (3 marks)

2 In what way did the baby look like a prune?
   b) She was small and wrinkled like a prune.   (2 marks)

3 How have the parents behaved since the new baby was born?
   c) They have paid no attention to their older daughter.   (2 marks)

4 Why does the girl say: "I wish she'd stop being a baby / and start being older than me"?
   b) She thinks the only way of getting any attention is to be the youngest child.   (2 marks)

5 Which pair of words rhymes?
   b) croon   prune   (2 marks)

6 What does "scarcely" mean in verse one?
   c) hardly   (2 marks)

7 What does "exclaim" mean in verse three?
   b) shout   (2 marks)

Extension activities

1 Do you feel sorry for the girl in the poem or do you think she is being selfish? Why?

2 Write a reply, giving advice to the parent who wrote the following letter.

> Dear Agony Aunt,
>
> Please help me! I just don't know what to do about my older daughter. Since my baby was born three weeks ago, she has been behaving so badly. She throws his food on the floor, kicks me and is horrible to the new baby. She says she wishes the baby would go and live in someone else's house.
> I am so busy with the new baby that I have no time to deal with a rude and sulky girl. What should I do?
>
> Yours sincerely
>
> J. Prelutsky

3 Some people think it is best to be any only child. Some people think it is wonderful to have lots of brothers and sisters. What do you think? Explain your answer.

SPECIFIC SKILLS	expressing and justifying an opinion; giving advice; writing a letter

Years of compulsory education

GENRE	information: chart
READING STRATEGIES	interpretation of a chart
QUESTION FORM	cloze
UNDERSTANDING TESTED	all questions – literal
CURRICULUM LINK	maths; geography

1 *In Italy children can leave school when they are <u>14</u> years old.* (1 mark)

2 *In the Netherlands and the United Kingdom children must go to school when they are <u>5</u> years old and can leave school when they are <u>16</u> years old.* (2 marks)

3 *In Ireland children can start school at the age of <u>4</u> but it is not compulsory until they are <u>6</u>.* (1 mark)

4 *Children in the United Kingdom have to attend school for <u>2</u> years more than children in Austria.* (1 mark)

5 *<u>Five</u> countries in the table have a leaving age of fifteen.* (1 mark)

6 *Compulsory education begins at the age of <u>6</u> or <u>7</u> years in most countries in the table.* (2 marks)

7 *In Portugal, children can start school at the age of <u>3</u> but it is not compulsory until they are <u>6</u>.* (1 mark)

8 *Most countries in the table have a leaving age of <u>16</u>.* (1 mark)

9 *In the United Kingdom, you can stay at school until the age of <u>18</u> if you want to.* (1 mark)

10 *In Sweden, children start school at the age of <u>7</u>.* (1 mark)

11 *Two countries offer two years of voluntary part-time education over the age of sixteen. They are <u>Belgium</u> and <u>Germany</u>.* (2 marks)

12 *Pupils in Switzerland have <u>9</u> years of compulsory education.* (1 mark)

Extension activities

1 Look at the table again. Write about which facts you find most surprising or interesting.

2 Do you think it is a good idea for children to go to playgroups and nursery school before they start school? Explain your answer.

3 Describe your first day at school.

4 "Your schooldays are the happiest days of your life." Do you agree? Why?

SPECIFIC SKILLS	interpreting graphical information; expressing an opinion; autobiographical writing

What is glass?

GENRE	information: report
READING STRATEGIES	skimming; scanning; detailed reading
QUESTION FORM	questions requiring answers in complete sentences
UNDERSTANDING TESTED	questions 1, 2 – literal; 3, 5, 6, 7 – deductive; 4 – inferential;
CURRICULUM LINK	science

1 Is it true that glass is really a liquid?
   Yes, it is true. (1 mark)

2 Write down six everyday glass objects that are mentioned in the passage.
   They are windows, mirrors, bottles, jars, lenses and television screens. (2 marks)

3 Think of four more everyday objects made of glass and write them down.
   *Accept any four sensible answers. Answers might include: light bulbs, drinking
   glasses, vases, fish bowls, paperweights, jewellery, etc.* (2 marks)

4 Explain why glass is a very unusual material. Give all the reasons you can find
   in the passage.
   *Reasons given in the passage are: it is strong; it is hard; it is transparent; it can be
   made into different shapes.* (2 marks)

5 What do the following words mean?
   "Brittle" means easily broken. (1 mark)
   "Transparent" means able to be seen through. (1 mark)
   "Properties" means characteristics or special qualities. (1 mark)

6 How many years are there in a century?
   There are 100 years in a century. (1 mark)

7 What is the difference between a discovery and an invention?
   *A discovery is finding something which already exists but which no-one knew
   about before. An invention is making something brand new which no-one
   has ever made before.* (2 + 2 marks)

Extension activities

1 Explain the differences between a telescope, a microscope and binoculars.

2 Explain the differences between a glazier, an optician and a glass-blower.

3 Use books in your class library to find out about how glass is made from sand (silica)
   and soda or potash. Write an account of what you find out.

SPECIFIC SKILLS	vocabulary; research and retrieval; writing an account

UNIT 23

Our playground

GENRE	poem
READING STRATEGIES	skimming; scanning; detailed reading
QUESTION FORM	multiple choice
UNDERSTANDING TESTED	questions 1, 3 – literal; 2, 4 – inferential; ; 5 – deductive
CURRICULUM LINK	PSHE

The true sentences are:

1b) *The playground in the poem is no good for playing football on because it slopes.* (3 marks)

2a) *The team that has to score at the top of the slope always loses.* (3 marks)

3b) *Both verses end with the same line.* (3 marks)

4b) *The poet thinks that life is like a game of football played on a sloping playground.* (3 marks)

5a) *In real life, the "Downhills" are lucky and successful people.* (3 marks)

Extension activities

1 Explain in your own words why the game of football described in the poem is not fair.

2 What would you suggest the players could do to make the game more fair?

3 Why do some people like football, and other people don't like it? Make a list of all the reasons you can think of for both points of view. List your ideas under the following two headings:

REASONS WHY SOME PEOPLE LIKE FOOTBALL	REASONS WHY SOME PEOPLE DON'T LIKE FOOTBALL

4 Make a list of all the games that people play on your school playground. Do a survey to find out which games are the most popular. Make a bar chart to display your findings.

SPECIFIC SKILLS	additional comprehension questions; making a list; considering opposing points of view; reflective writing; conducting a survey; presenting information as a bar chart

Boy attacked by mastiff

GENRE	information: report (newspaper article)
READING STRATEGIES	skimming; scanning; detailed reading
QUESTION FORM	true/false
UNDERSTANDING TESTED	all questions – literal
CURRICULUM LINK	PSHE

The true statements are:

1 *Mark Davison was ten years old when the dog attacked him.*   (3 marks)

4 *The dog has now been destroyed.*   (3 marks)

6 *Mark was injured on his face, chest and arms.*   (3 marks)

10 *The dog that attacked Mark bit its owner too.*   (3 marks)

13 *Mark received treatment at Middlesbrough General Hospital.*   (3 marks)

Extension activities

1 List the statements that are false (2, 3, 5, 7, 8, 9, 11, 12) and explain exactly why each one is inaccurate or untrue.

2 Write a newspaper article about yourself achieving something wonderful. Make up a suitable headline. Quote somebody's words of praise about you!

3 Have you ever been in hospital or been to visit someone in hospital? Describe the occasion. Include in your description any sights, sounds, smells and sensations you still remember.

4 Imagine the following letter was printed in the same newspaper the next day. Would you agree or disagree with the person who wrote the letter? Write a letter back to the person, explaining what you think and why.

Dear Editor,

I was deeply shocked to read about the boy who was attacked and injured by a dangerous bull mastiff dog. If I had my way, every dog in the country would be destroyed immediately. Dogs are vicious animals and are quite unsuitable as pets.

Yours faithfully,

F. Carter.

SPECIFIC SKILLS	additional comprehension questions; writing a newspaper article; descriptive writing; letter-writing

Albert changes schools

GENRE	fiction: realistic (issues); significant author
READING STRATEGIES	skimming; scanning; detailed reading
QUESTION FORM	questions requiring answers in complete sentences
UNDERSTANDING TESTED	questions 1, 3 – literal; 5 – deductive; 2, 4, 6 – inferential
CURRICULUM LINK	PSHE

1 Why had Albert's mother decided they had to move to the town?
They had to move to the town for her to find work. (2 marks)

2 Why was Albert nicknamed Twiddler?
He was nicknamed Twiddler because when he was nervous he twiddled his hair. (2 marks)

3 Where did Albert go to try to hide from the other children?
He went behind the bike shed in the school playground. (2 marks)

4 Why did Albert smile and laugh so much at his new school?
He smiled and laughed because he wanted to seem friendly so that people would like him. (3 marks)

5 How do you dribble a ball?
You dribble a ball by giving it lots of little kicks to keep it moving along the ground as you run along with it. (3 marks)

6 Why did Sid tell his friends to watch while he told Albert the story about his father?
He told them to watch because he wanted them to have fun at Albert's expense.
He wanted them to see how he could make Albert believe any silly story. (3 marks)

Extension activities

1 Explain why Albert found it so difficult to get used to his new school.

2 The passage says that Albert had a "thatch" of hair. Explain what his hair had in common with a thatched roof.

3 At the end of each day, Albert felt "like a sponge squeezed dry". Explain how this comparison helps us to understand how Albert felt.

4 Have you ever changed schools? Did you find it easy to settle down and make friends? Explain what you found easy and what you found difficult.

5 Sid Creedy is a bit of a bully. He enjoys making Albert look silly. Write about the things that bullies do to make their victims feel really miserable, and about what someone can do if he or she is being bullied.

SPECIFIC SKILLS	additional comprehension questions; reflective writing; similes and metaphors

Dilly Dinosaur, Detective

GENRE	fiction: fantasy; mystery
READING STRATEGIES	skimming; scanning; detailed reading
QUESTION FORM	questions requiring answers in complete sentences
UNDERSTANDING TESTED	question 1 – literal; 3, 5, 6, 7, 8 – deductive; 2, 4 – inferential
CURRICULUM LINK	English

1 What was Dilly pretending to be?
Dilly was pretending to be a detective / Inspector Duff. (1 mark)

2 Did Dilly explain why he was asking so many questions?
Yes, he did explain in the end. (1 mark)

3 What is "TV" short for?
"TV" is short for television. (1 mark)

4 How did the family feel about being asked questions?
The family felt annoyed / puzzled / impatient. (1 mark)

5 Why was it silly for Dilly to ask the family what their address was and where they had been on their holidays?
It was silly because he already knew the answers to the questions. (2 marks)

6 Which word in paragraph four means "in the end"?
"Finally" means "in the end". (1 mark)

7 Which word in the last paragraph tells us that "Inspector Duff, Dinosaur Detective" is a series of programmes and not just one programme?
The word "episode" tells us that it is a series. (1 mark)

8 What do the following words mean?
a) *"Pester" means keep on asking the same questions in an annoying way.* (1 mark)
b) *"Devious" means sly, or trying to do something in an indirect, secretive way.* (1 mark)
c) *"Investigating" means finding out about something.* (1 mark)
d) *"Solve" means find the answer to a puzzle or problem.* (1 mark)
e) *"Occasionally" means sometimes or not very often.* (1 mark)
f) *"Unmask" means reveal or expose.* (1 mark)
g) *"Villain" means a criminal.* (1 mark)

Extension activities

Use a dictionary to find out the exact meaning of the following words.

1 interrogate	3 confess	5 investigate
2 deny	4 contradict	6 imply

SPECIFIC SKILLS	extending vocabulary; using a dictionary

Life in a castle

GENRE	information: report
READING STRATEGIES	skimming; scanning; detailed reading
QUESTION FORM	questions requiring answers in complete sentences
UNDERSTANDING TESTED	questions 1, 2, 4, 7, 9 – literal; 3, 5, 6, 10 – inferential; 8 – deductive
CURRICULUM LINK	history

1 What were the two main uses of a castle?
A castle was a fortress and it was also a home. (1 mark)

2 What was used to cover the floor?
The floor was covered with rushes or straw. (1 mark)

3 What furniture would you find in the Great Hall?
You would find tables, benches, wooden stools, storage chests and maybe a few chairs. (2 marks)

4 Where did most people sleep?
Most people slept on straw mattresses on the floor. (1 mark)

5 How was having a bath different from in our times?
If you wanted a bath there were no baths with pipes and taps. The water had to be heated and poured into a wooden tub. There might be curtains to pull around the tub. (2 marks)

6 There were no flush toilets in a castle. Explain how the castle lavatories worked.
The lavatories were in small rooms built into the outside wall. There was a stone seat and the sewage went down a chute and fell into a moat, river or pit below. (2 marks)

7 What is another word used in the passage that means"lavatory" or "toilet"?
The word "garderobe" means "lavatory". (2 marks)

8 What does "a portable brazier" mean?
It means a fire basket that could be moved around. (2 marks)

9 Why did ceilings have to be high in the days when fires were in the centre of the room?
The ceilings had to be high to allow room for the smoke to circulate. (1 mark)

10 Write down two ways in which the lord of the castle and his wife lived a more comfortable life than other people in the castle.
They had the most comfortable chairs to sit on. They had a bed to sleep on. (1 mark)

Extension activities

Use the clues and complete the words. (They are all to do with castles.)

1 a deep ditch filled with water to keep invaders out: **m** _ _ _

2 a strong, spiked gate that could be raised or lowered: **p** _ _ _ _ _ _ _ _ _

3 a wall on top of a tower with spaces to shoot arrows through: **b** _ _ _ _ _ _ _ _ _

4 a bridge that could be pulled up to stop invaders getting in: **d** _ _ _ _ _ _ _ _ _

5 an underground cell where prisoners were kept: **d** _ _ _ _ _ _

SPECIFIC SKILLS	extending subject-specific vocabulary

GENRE	information: report
READING STRATEGIES	skimming; scanning; detailed reading
QUESTION FORM	questions requiring answers in complete sentences; true/false
UNDERSTANDING TESTED	questions 1, 2, 3, 4, 5 – literal; 6, 7 – deductive
CURRICULUM LINK	science

1 What do hedgehogs do when they are scared?
They curl up into a ball. (1 mark)

2 Give two reasons why desert hedgehogs in Africa and Asia dig burrows in the sand.
They dig burrows to get away from the hot sun and to hide from their enemies. (2 marks)

3 What two things can a hedgehog tell about another hedgehog just by its smell?
A hedgehog can tell the age and sex of another hedgehog just by its smell. (2 marks)

4 Make a list of four facts about a hedgehog's spines that you learn from the passage.
Facts mentioned in the passage are: Each spine is about 22 mm long. Older hedgehogs have more spines than younger ones. The spines of old hedgehogs are often damaged. The spines of young hedgehogs are shiny and in good condition. A hedgehog uses a special set of muscles to raise and lower its spines. (4 marks)

5 The true sentences are:
c) Hedgehogs cannot see very well. (1 mark)
f) Hedgehogs are mammals. (1 mark)
h) Hedgehogs curl up by tightening special muscles. (1 mark)

6 What do the following words mean?
a) "Damaged" means broken or injured. (0.5 mark)
b) "Desert" means a very dry area of the world. (0.5 mark)
c) "Mammal" means a creature which gives birth to live young and feeds them on milk. (0.5 mark)

7 Give the opposites of the following words.
a) The opposite of "different" is "same". (0.5 mark)
b) The opposite of "raise" is "lower". (0.5 mark)
c) The opposite of "old" is "young". (0.5 mark)

Extension activities

1 If you have ever seen a hedgehog, describe what it looked like and where and when you saw it.

2 Imagine that you are a hedgehog. You live in a garden with lots of bushes. A strange dog suddenly rushes towards you and barks. What do you do? Write an account of what happens from the hedgehog's point of view.

3 Use books in your class library to find out more about hedgehogs. Write a report of what you find out.

SPECIFIC SKILLS	describing an experience; imaginative writing; research and retrieval; writing a report

Helen Keller

GENRE	information: biography; recount
READING STRATEGIES	skimming; scanning; detailed reading
QUESTION FORM	true/false
UNDERSTANDING TESTED	all questions – literal
CURRICULUM LINK	history

The true sentences are:

1   *Helen Keller was blind and deaf when Anne Sullivan came to live with her.*   *(3 marks)*

5   *Sign language is a language you talk with your hands.*   *(3 marks)*

7   *Anne taught Helen to read and write in Braille.*   *(3 marks)*

8   *Helen eventually learned to speak.*   *(3 marks)*

12   *Helen did a great deal in her life to help other blind people.*   *(3 marks)*

Extension activities

1 Rewrite the false sentences from the book, changing them to make them true (sentences 2, 3, 4, 6, 9, 10 and 11).

2 Make a list of the main facts that you learn about Helen Keller in the passage.

3 Make a list of the main facts that you learn about Anne Sullivan in the passage.

4 What do the following words and phrases mean?

  a) fever
  b) to spoil someone
  c) Braille
  d) furious
  e) patient
  f) famous
  g) encourage

5 Write a story about a character who found it difficult to do something but succeeded in the end.

6 Use books in your class library to find out about the life of Louis Braille, who invented the Braille system of writing. Write an account of what you find out.

7 Find out more about Braille writing and make a chart showing the Braille pattern for each letter of the alphabet.

SPECIFIC SKILLS	rewriting false sentences as true; making a list; writing a story; vocabulary; research and retrieval; presenting information in a different format

GENRE	fiction: animal
READING STRATEGIES	skimming; scanning; detailed reading
QUESTION FORM	questions requiring answers in complete sentences
UNDERSTANDING TESTED	questions 1, 2, 6 – literal; 3, 4, 5 – inferential; 8, 9 – evaluative; 7, 10 – deductive
CURRICULUM LINK	geography

1 Why were the kittens called One, Two and Three?
*They were given these names just for the time being, before they went to their
new homes.* *(1.5 marks)*

2 How can you tell that One was really frightened when he heard Prince barking?
You can tell that One was frightened because his legs shook. *(1.5 marks)*

3 Is Two a female kitten?
We can't tell from this passage whether Two was a male or a female kitten. *(1.5 marks)*

4 Why couldn't the kittens see?
The kittens couldn't see because they had only just been born. *(1.5 marks)*

5 What had been put in the box to make it cosy for Minnie and her kittens?
Some straw had been put in the box to make it cosy. *(1.5 marks)*

6 What noise did the river make in the storm?
The river roared in the storm. *(1.5 marks)*

7 Which word in the passage means "cosy"?
"Snug" means "cosy". *(1.5 marks)*

8 Which word best describes Minnie?
"Protective" describes Minnie best. *(1.5 marks)*

9 Which word best describes the kittens?
"Timid" describes the kittens best. *(1.5 marks)*

10 What is the plural of "lady"?
The plural of "lady" is "ladies". *(1.5 marks)*

Extension activities

1 In what ways was Minnie a good mother to the kittens?

2 What things couldn't the new-born kittens do?

3 What evidence is there that the shed was hardly ever used?

4 Make a list of all the sounds that the kittens could hear.

5 Mother cats always find a safe, private place to have their kittens. Ask someone
whose cat has had kittens about the place their cat chose, and write about
what you find out.

SPECIFIC SKILLS	additional comprehension questions; finding out and writing up

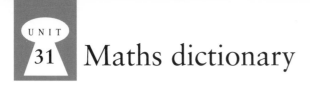

UNIT 31 Maths dictionary

GENRE	alphabetical text: dictionary
READING STRATEGIES	skimming; scanning; detailed reading
QUESTION FORM	sentence completion
UNDERSTANDING TESTED	question 5 – literal; 1, 3, 6, 7, 8, 9 – deductive; 2, 4 – inferential
CURRICULUM LINK	geography

1 *If "perpendicular" had been included in this dictionary, it would have come between* <u>*"percentage"*</u> *and* <u>*"place value"*</u>. (2 marks)

2 *In Miss Woolacott's class there are 30 children. Fifteen of them have brown hair. So* <u>*50%*</u> *of the class has brown hair.* (2 marks)

3 *Just two of these numbers are prime numbers: 5, 15, 17, 21, 84 and 100. The two prime numbers are* <u>*5*</u> *and* <u>*17*</u>. (2 marks)

4 *Two examples of numbers in a pattern are given. The next number after 19 in the first example would be* <u>*21*</u>. (1 mark)

5 *A pentagon has* <u>*five*</u> *sides.* (1 mark)

6 *The product of 4 and 2 is* <u>*8*</u>. (1 mark)

7 *"Analysing" a pattern means* <u>*working it out/working out the sequence*</u>. (2 marks)

8 *"Maths" is an abbreviation of* <u>*mathematics*</u>. (2 marks)

9 *The opposite of "solid" is* <u>*"hollow"*</u>. (2 marks)

Extension activities

1 Arrange these terms in alphabetical order for another dictionary page:
   a) rhombus, recurring, ratio, right angle, reduce, round up, rectangle
   b) sphere, solution, square, scalene, symbol, symmetry, sequence

2 What is the difference between a dictionary, a glossary and an index?

3 List ten prime numbers.

4 How many sides do these figures have?
   a) a triangle
   b) a rectangle
   c) a hexagon
   d) an octagon
   e) a rhombus

SPECIFIC SKILLS	alphabetical order; vocabulary work

GENRE	play (raising issues)
READING STRATEGIES	skimming; scanning; detailed reading
QUESTION FORM	questions requiring answers in complete sentences
UNDERSTANDING TESTED	questions 2, 3 – deductive; 1, 4, 5, 6, 7, 8 – inferential; 9 – evaluative
CURRICULUM LINK	citizenship

1 How do we know that Barry Hunter has bullied people before?
We know from the comments of the class that he is in the habit of picking on people and making them cry. We can also tell from the class discussion after he has gone that it is a problem that has been going on for a while. (1 mark)

2 Why do the rest of the class whisper when Barry is around?
They probably whisper because they are frightened of him and don't want him to hear.
(1 mark)

3 Why does the nickname "Moving Mountain" hurt Penny so much?
Penny is probably plumper than the other girls and this nickname makes her feel ugly. (2 marks)

4 Mark has poor eyesight. Mention two of Barry's cruel remarks about this.
Accept any two of these: his glasses are as thick as bottle ends; he has bionic eyes; he can't catch a ball; he can't save a goal; (possibly) he doesn't look human. (2 marks)

5 If Penny's big sister advised her to keep out of Barry Hunter's way, what do you think Penny's answer would be?
Penny would say that she does keep out of his way and it makes no difference. She also tells him to go away and he won't. (2 marks)

6 Mark's big brother would probably tell him that Barry wouldn't bully him if he stood up for himself. Do you think he is right in this case?
Mark tells Barry to go away and he also lashes out at him. He misses and Barry just laughs. (2 marks)

7 Which two adults mentioned here probably think that children should sort out these problems by themselves?
The two adults are the caretaker and the dinner lady. (2 marks)

8 One adult mentioned here would probably tell Mark that it was his own fault that he was bullied. What is his name?
His name is Mr. Fairway. (1 mark)

9 If you were there, what would your advice be?
Reward any thoughtful suggestions. (2 marks)

Extension activities

1 What advice would you give to Penny and Mark to stop Barry Turner bullying them again?

2 Does your school have a policy for dealing with bullies? What is it?

SPECIFIC SKILLS	more advanced comprehension questions; personal writing

Computer health

GENRE	information: persuasive text (advice)
READING STRATEGIES	skimming; scanning; detailed reading
QUESTION FORM	true/false
UNDERSTANDING TESTED	questions 2, 5 – literal; 1, 3, 4, 6, 7 – inferential
CURRICULUM LINK	ICT

Write out the sentence from each pair that is true.

1 *b) It is sometimes advisable to wear sunglasses when working on a computer.* (2 marks)

2 *b) You should rest your eyes by looking away from the screen every ten minutes or so.* (2 marks)

3 *b) When you are sitting at a keyboard, always make sure that your elbows are level with the keyboard.* (2 marks)

4 *a) Shrugging your shoulders can help to reduce the strain in your back.* (2 marks)

5 *b) Keeping your wrists flat as you type is the safest way of typing.* (2 marks)

6 *b) Using a mouse every day can cause repetitive strain syndrome.* (2 marks)

7 *b) It is possible to use computers safely.* (2 marks)

(+ 1 bonus mark if all questions attempted)

Extension activities

1 What is the meaning of the underlined words?
   a) follow some simple <u>guidelines</u>
   b) <u>focus</u> your eyes
   c) at <u>regular intervals</u>
   d) <u>symptoms</u> similar to arthritis
   e) shake your hands to relieve <u>tension</u>

2 Ask a friend to sit working at a computer. Look at his/her posture and write a report. Use these headings:
   - back
   - elbows
   - wrists
   - feet
   (Give your report a heading, and sign and date it at the end.)

3 Make a poster for the wall near the computer(s), giving five safety rules.

4 One of your friends at another school has never used a computer and thinks they are a waste of time. Write a letter to him/her saying what you think.

SPECIFIC SKILLS	vocabulary; report writing from observation; poster (summary); letter writing; expressing a viewpoint

Poetry in different forms

GENRE	poems (haiku, limerick, shape)
READING STRATEGIES	skimming; scanning; detailed reading
QUESTION FORM	questions requiring answers in complete sentences; sentence completion
UNDERSTANDING TESTED	questions 1, 2, 6, 8 – literal; 5 – inferential; 3, 4 – deductive; 7 – evaluative
CURRICULUM LINK	music

1 Look again at the haiku. How many syllables are there in it altogether?
There are seventeen syllables altogether.   (1 mark)

2 Complete this sentence and write it out.
*Line 1 of a haiku has <u>five</u> syllables, line 2 has <u>seven</u> syllables and line 3 has
<u>five</u> syllables.*   (3 marks)

3 In what sense do the sopranos in the haiku "soar"?
*The voices of the sopranos are higher than the voices of the other singers, and so
soar above them.*   (1 mark)

4   In what sense do the rest of the choir keep their "feet on the ground"?
*The rest of the choir have deeper voices than the sopranos, so it as if they do not
soar into the air with them.*   (1 mark)

5 A limerick has five lines. Which lines rhyme with each other?
Lines 1, 2 and 5 rhyme, and lines 3 and 4 rhyme.   (2 marks)

6 Write out the shape poem, "A Cello", as an 8-line poem.
*My cello big and fat / makes the sound of a screeching rat. / It plays F double sharp /
when I want it to play B flat. / It sounds like a bad composition / when I play in the
4th position. / If I try to play vibrato / my bow goes all s-t-a-c-c-ato!*   (3 marks)

7 Which do you like best, the 8-line version or the one in the shape of a cello?
Give at least two reasons for your verdict.
*Open. Reward any reasoned response, one mark for each reason. Here are some
possible answers: / I like the 8-line poem best because it is: / easier to understand. /
easier to read aloud. / easier to enjoy the rhymes.*

*I like the shape poem best because: / it cleverly fits the shape of the cello. / of its witty
use of the final punctuation mark. / of its clever use of s-t-a-c-c- in one line and ato in
the next (you can almost hear the screech). / it is a pleasure to look at. / of its relevance
of subject to shape.*   (2 marks)

8 Use your dictionary to find the meaning of these two words in "A Cello":
a) **vibrato**   b) **staccato**
*"Vibrato" is a slight trembling in a note to make it sound richer and fuller.
"Staccato" means short and sharp.*   (2 marks)

Extension activities

1 Write this sentence as a haiku:
Silent now and still, the music room is empty of notes and pupils.
a) What does it gain from being written as a haiku?
b) Continue the "story" in the haiku by writing a second haiku to follow it.

2 Draw the shape of a guitar, a trumpet or a harp and write a shape poem inside it.

SPECIFIC SKILLS	modelling own poems; continuing the story; expressing and justifying a response

Dear Householder

GENRE	information: explanation (letter)
READING STRATEGIES	skimming; scanning; detailed reading
QUESTION FORM	true/false
UNDERSTANDING TESTED	statements 1, 6 – literal; 7, 9, 10 – deductive; 3, 11 – inferential
CURRICULUM LINK	citizenship

These statements are true:

1 *The blue bins have not yet been delivered to householders.*   *(2 marks)*

3 *Damp paper should not be put in the blue bins.*   *(2 marks)*

6 *Plastic carrier bags should not be put in the blue bins but plastic bottles can be.*   *(2 marks)*

7 *Potato peelings and grass cuttings can be used to make compost.*   *(2 marks)*

9 *Recycling means changing waste products into something that can be used again.*   *(2 marks)*

10 *Jars and glass bottles can be recycled but they should not be put in the blue bin.*   *(2 marks)*

11 *The Council is proud that less waste will have to be buried in landfill sites.*   *(2 marks)*

(+ 1 bonus mark for careful writing)

Extension activities

1 Most councils now have recycling schemes. Find out what is collected for recycling in your area and what the collecting arrangements are.

2 Does your school have a recycling policy? If it has, what does the school save for recycling?

3 Did you know that a baby probably uses 5000 disposable nappies before he or she is toilet-trained? Each household throws away nearly 2.5kg of plastic wrappings a year. How can we reduce the amount of waste we have to dispose of? Do you have any good ideas?

4 Have you ever made good use of something that would otherwise have been thrown away? Describe this example of recycling!

5 Explain how recycling helps the environment.

SPECIFIC SKILLS	research and reporting; contributing own ideas; describing something made; evaluation

GENRE	poem from another culture (Africa)
READING STRATEGIES	skimming; scanning; detailed reading
QUESTION FORM	questions requiring answers in complete sentences
UNDERSTANDING TESTED	questions 5a, 7a – literal; 4 – deductive; 1, 2, 3, 6 – inferential; 5b, 7b – evaluative
CURRICULUM LINK	geography

1 Why do you think the writer has "walked miles"?
   The writer has walked miles looking for water.   *(2 marks)*

2 Why are the lines describing the drought very short and jerky?
   *These lines suggest exhaustion/desperation/despair/the state of mind of the people
   suffering from the drought.*   *(2 marks)*

3 a) Which three words are used to describe the sound of the rain on the rooftops?
   The three words are: tapping, pitter and pattering.   *(1 mark)*
   b) Which two letters in these words make the same sound as the raindrops?
   The two letters/consonants "p" and "t" sound like the raindrops.   *(1 mark)*

4 What is another word for "pails"?
   Another word for pails is "buckets".   *(1 mark)*

5 a) Which line in the second verse is repeated?
   The line "The sound of rain" is repeated.   *(1 mark)*
   b) If you were reading this poem to the class, how would you say this line?
   I would say it joyfully/with relief in my voice.   *(1 mark)*

6 The family are very happy now that it has started to rain after the long drought.
   Mention three things that they don't have to worry about now.
   *They don't have to worry about finding water to drink, and having water for washing.
   And there will be grass now for the cattle.*   *(3 marks)*

7 a) What clue are we given that the poet may be describing a childhood memory?
   The poet's gap between the teeth suggests early childhood.   *(1 mark)*
   b) If it is a childhood memory, why has the poet chosen to write about it in the
   present tense?
   The present tense makes it more vivid/suggests it is happening at this very moment.   *(2 marks)*

Extension activities

1 What is your earliest memory of bad weather – perhaps heavy snow or
  floods, or thunder and lightning? Write about it, describing how you felt.

2 Write a poem about the weather you like best.

3 Prepare a performance of "Drought" with six friends. Some of the group can
  say the poem and the others can mime to the words. Take care to convey the
  changing mood in the poem.

4 Write a story where the weather plays an important part.

SPECIFIC SKILLS	personal writing; writing a poem; preparing a performance; mime; narrative writing

UNIT 37 Evacuation

GENRE	fiction: historical
READING STRATEGIES	skimming; scanning; detailed reading
QUESTION FORM	questions requiring answers in complete sentences
UNDERSTANDING TESTED	questions 3, 5, 7, 9 – literal; 10 – deductive; 1, 2, 4, 8 – inferential; 6 – evaluative
CURRICULUM LINK	history

1 What special reason does David have for trying to be brave?
*David wants to be as brave as his father. His father has been killed in the war,
and now he is the man of the family.* *(2 marks)*

2 What may have happened in Battersea to cause the "glow of fire" in the sky?
A bomb has probably fallen. *(1 mark)*

3 How did Brian Perkins die?
He died with the rest of his family when his house was bombed. *(1 mark)*

4 Why is David's school being evacuated to the country?
*His school is being evacuated (like many others) because it is getting too dangerous
to stay in London.* *(2 marks)*

5 How many pupils in David's class are staying behind in London?
No pupils are staying behind. Everyone is going. *(1 mark)*

6 Which one of these adjectives best describes how David's mother feels about his
going away? Why?
angry   amused   relieved   impatient
*"Relieved" best describes how she feels. She doesn't want him to be killed like
her husband.* *(2 marks)*

7 What is Tony Tucker's nickname?
His nickname is Tucky. *(1 mark)*

8 How does David feel about leaving London and his mother?
He wishes he could stay but he knows that he can't. *(1 mark)*

9 David has two items of luggage. What are they?
He has his case and his gas mask. *(2 marks)*

10 Explain the meaning of the underlined words:
She <u>chucked</u> him under the chin.
Miss Evers' voice rang out <u>above the hubbub</u>.
"Chucked" means patted or tapped lightly. *(1 mark)*
"Above the hubbub" means above all the noise of people talking at the same time. *(1 mark)*

Extension activities

1 Imagine you are David's mother. Write the letter that she promised to send him.

2 Do you agree with David's mother that boys and men shouldn't cry?

3 Talk to an elderly neighbour or relation about their memories of the Second
World War. Prepare a list of questions and after the interview, write a report.
Alternatively, record your interview and play it to the class.

SPECIFIC SKILLS	letter writing; writing in role; preparing a list; interviewing; writing a report